HOW TO SELL CARS

The Art of the Dealership

BRIAN L. VIERS
Author of Significant U

© 2025 Brian L. Viers

All rights reserved. No part of this publication may be reproduced, distributed, or transmitted in any form or by any means, including photocopying, recording, or other electronic or mechanical methods, without the prior written permission of the publisher, except in the case of brief quotations used for educational purposes or reviews.

For permission requests, please contact:
brianviers.com

Published in the United States of America.

Cover design, layout, and interior formatting by Sharon Viers.

This workbook is designed to provide practical guidance for sales professionals. While every effort has been made to ensure accuracy, the author and publisher disclaim any liability for damages incurred directly or indirectly from the use or application of the contents of this book. Individual results may vary based on effort, market conditions, and other variables.

ISBN: 978-0-9996072-9-9

How to Sell Cars: The Art of the Dealership

First Edition | 2025

Significant U Resource Series

This book is one of several transformative tools developed under the *Significant U* initiative, a comprehensive framework designed to equip individuals and organizations to live, lead, and grow with purpose.

Created to complement the core messages found in *7 Steps to Becoming Simply Significant*, this resource is intended to deepen your reflection, sharpen your execution, and expand your impact.

The Significant U Resource Series includes:
- *7 Steps to Becoming Simply Significant* Book
- Interactive Workbooks and Planning Templates
- Online Courses and Video Modules
- Coaching Tools and Assessment Guides
- Seminars, Workshops, and Speaking Engagements
- Business & Personal Development Planners

TABLE OF CONTENTS

Chapter or Section Title	Page
Introduction	1
Chapter 1: The Shift That Changes Everything	7
Chapter 2: Listening is Selling	16
Chapter 3: Presenting the Right Vehicle	26
Chapter 4: Finding the Buyers	37
Chapter 5: Overcoming Objections	49
Chapter 6: Closing with Confidence	57
Chapter 7: Becoming a Lifetime Advisor	66
Chapter 8: Building a Business Inside the Business	72
Chapter 9: Creating Raving Fans (Not Just Customers)	80

Chapter 10: Leveraging Technology for Sales Success	88
Chapter 11: Building Your Personal Brand as a Sales Professional	99
Chapter 12: Mastering the Art of Closing the Deal	106
Chapter 13: Building Long-Term Relationships for Repeat Business	114
Chapter 14: Leveraging Social Media for Sales Success	122
Chapter 15: Mastering the Test Drive	132
Chapter 16: Overcoming Objections and Closing the Deal	137
Bonus Chapter: Master the Follow-Up—Forever	145
Closing Chapter: The Daily Commitment to Mastery	152
30-Day Sales Challenge: Building Lasting Habits and Accountability	159

Introduction

Welcome to the *How to Sell Cars: The Art of the Dealership.*

You don't just sell cars, you build trust, solve problems, and guide people through one of the biggest purchases of their lives. This book is here to help you do it better.

I began my career in the automotive industry in 1991, working with Chevrolet, Hyundai, and RV dealerships in Bradley, Illinois. From day one, I was driven to understand not just how to sell—but also serve, and why people buy. I dove deep into the behavioral patterns of both buyers and sellers, uncovering insights that would shape the way I approached every conversation.

Over the years, I developed a system rooted in these behavioral principles—one that doesn't just push for the sale, but builds long-term trust, loyalty, and success. It's a system that redefines what it means to serve, and it's helped me build and lead teams that consistently exceed expectations.

Now, with over 30 years of entrepreneurship and business development experience, I've turned those insights into practical, easy-to-use tools through

Significant U Resources. In *Upper Hand: How the Dealer Always Wins*, I discussed and shared the real strategies that allow dealerships and salespeople to operate with integrity at peak performance, while always putting the customer relationship first. Now specifically for the salesperson comes *How to Sell Cars: The Art of the Dealership*, and when aligned properly will provide unimaginable results and values.

This isn't about gimmicks. It's about gaining the advantage through listening and then understanding. And once you learn how to truly serve, you'll discover why the dealer, done right, always wins.

Whether your brand new to the automotive sales industry or a seasoned pro looking to sharpen your edge, this is designed to help you build sustainable success grounded in trust, authenticity, and consistency.

This isn't about outdated, high-pressure sales tactics or memorized scripts. Instead, it's about developing skills that last, relationships that convert, and values that scale. Each page is built to help you hit the ground running and improve the effectiveness of every customer interaction.

Inside, you'll find powerful tools and techniques you can immediately apply, including:

- Step-by-Step Sales Process Guides

    Master each phase of the customer journey—from greeting to follow-up. These guides provide a structured approach to selling without sacrificing personal style, helping you stay focused and effective whether you're managing multiple leads or assisting walk-in customers.

    Use Case: Role-play the sales process with a team member to build muscle memory and confidence.

- Buyer Behavior Insights

    Understand what today's customers are thinking, feeling, and needing. By identifying buying signals and customer personalities, you'll tailor your approach to meet people where they are—not where you want them to be.

    Use Case: Apply customer profiling exercises to quickly identify decision drivers and hesitation points.

- Real-World Objection Handling Strategies

    Get equipped with real examples of how to handle common objections without sounding defensive or forceful. These strategies help you listen, empathize, and guide the conversation toward a solution.

    Use Case: Practice overcoming the "I need to think about it" objection using techniques provided in this section.

- Relationship-Building Techniques

    Great salespeople don't close deals, they open relationships. Learn how to build rapport, earn trust, and connect on a human level to become a go-to resource rather than just another salesperson.

    Use Case: Implement the 3-Question Rapport Builder before diving into product features.

- Practical Tools for Follow-Up, Retention, and Referrals

    Success doesn't stop after the sale. Discover proven methods to keep the conversation going, earn repeat business, and turn satisfied customers into referral champions.

    Use Case: Create a 30-day post-sale follow-up calendar personalized to each buyer.

- Team Exercises and Discussion Prompts

    Designed for dealerships that want to build a culture of excellence, these exercises encourage teams to collaborate, reflect, and improve together. Perfect for sales meetings, onboarding sessions, or skill refreshers.

    Use Case: Use the "Customer Experience Scorecard" as a team to identify strengths and blind spots.

Tool / Section	Where to Find It
Step-by-Step Sales Process Guides	Chapters 1, 4, 5, 8
Buyer Behavior Insights	Chapter 2
Real-World Objection Handling Strategies	Chapters 5, 6, 16
Relationship-Building Techniques	Chapters 3, 7, 13
Practical Tools for Follow-Up, Retention, and Referrals	Chapters 8, 9, Bonus Chapter
Team Exercises and Discussion Prompts	Throughout (Maven Moves) + Bonus Chapter

Chapter 1
The Shift That Changes Everything

"We're not just selling cars—we're building legacies on wheels."

There's a reason you picked up this guide.
Maybe you're new to the lot, still wearing the tread off your first pair of dealership shoes. Maybe you're a veteran of the blacktop, but lately you've caught yourself wondering: *Is there a better way?*

A better way to sell. A better way to build a career. A better way to make a difference while making a living. If you've been in the automotive world for even a minute, you know the stereotypes: overly aggressive and always angling for the close. It's a reputation that's lingered for decades —the "car salesman" image that causes people to become uncomfortable, and maybe even put up a defense mechanism the moment they realize what you do for a living, thinking they are about to be "sold".

You've seen the cautious looks. You might have even fought to prove that you're different. Together, let's break this paradigm.

Here's the truth:
The future belongs to the salesperson who rewrites that story.

Today's most successful professionals aren't just selling cars — they're building relationships, creating loyal communities, and leading with values that customers can trust.

They're not chasing buyers down the lot.
They're attracting believers to their brand.
They're not just closing deals — they're opening doors to repeat business, referrals, and reputation.
They're advancing their craft with ongoing education, refining their skills like true professionals — not leaving it to chance, pressure, or luck.

This workbook isn't just about teaching you *how* to sell better — it's about resetting your entire mindset about *why* you sell.

When you change your perspective, you change your performance.
And when you build your approach on **trust, connection, and credibility**, you won't just be remembered — you'll be recommended.

The Maven Maker: Transforming Car Sales with Trust, Value, and Vision

Maven *(noun): A person who has special knowledge or experience; an expert.*

Becoming a Maven in your market means being the expert customers seek out — and are excited to talk about and share their newfound knowledge or experience.

It means your name becomes synonymous with integrity, reliability, and excellence.
It means you're no longer "just" a salesperson — you're a trusted advisor, a guide, a go-to name in your community.

And the best part?
When you reach this level of expertise and authenticity,

your customers do your marketing for you.

Every positive review, every recommendation, every story they tell their friends — it all becomes free, organic, powerful promotion.

You become your own brand.

How This Workbook Will Equip You

You will learn how to:
- Hear what your buyers aren't saying — and answer what they *truly* need.
- Become the trusted expert in your community — both inside and outside the showroom.
- Deliver unforgettable value — so buyers talk about *you*, not just the car.
- Build a book of business that stands strong through market shifts and economic changes.
- Turn every sale into a story worth sharing — making you *the Maven Maker* they can't forget.

This is bigger than one sale, one commission, or one good month.

This is about building a career — one fueled by reputation, referrals, and repeat success.

Once you understand the principles in this guide, you will never walk into a showroom the same way again.
It's time to change the perception.
It's time to rewrite the playbook.
It's time to become the kind of professional even if the skeptics can't help but trust.

Know the Buyer, Not Just the Car

It's easy to think that success in automotive sales is about knowing every model, every trim level, every tech package, and every financing incentive.
And yes — product knowledge is important.
But truly successful sales professionals know this secret:

You don't sell the car first. You sell the connection.
The most powerful tool in your sales toolbox isn't your vehicle inventory — it's your ability to *know the buyer*.
Not every buyer walks onto the lot the same way.
Some arrive with a spreadsheet of comparisons and questions ready to go.

Others drift in impulsively, attracted by your newest model up on display gleaming under the lights.

Some walk cautiously, reluctant, convinced they're "just looking."

Your job isn't to treat them all the same, it's to read them, understand them, and adapt to them.

Understanding Buyer Types

Here's a quick map of the most common buyer profiles you'll encounter:

The Researcher
- Comes armed with information: specs, pricing, competitors.
- Wants validation, not pressure.
- Respects those who can build *on top* of what they know, not undermine it.

   Strategy:
   - Respect their preparation.
   - Offer additional value or insights they may have missed.
   - Become their trusted expert, not their competitor.

The Emotional Buyer
- Buys with the heart first, brain second.

- Drawn to lifestyle, appearance, and feelings of status, freedom, or joy.

  Strategy:
  - Sell the *experience*, not just the features.

  - Paint pictures: "Imagine taking this on a road trip with your family."

  - Tap into the emotions that led them to your lot.

The Budget-Conscious Buyer
- Focuses on smart, affordable choices.

- Values long-term savings and practicality over luxury or flash.

  Strategy:
  - Lead with value propositions and cost-saving features.

  - Present practical packages, reliable models, and warranty benefits.

The Trade-In Negotiator
- Focused on maximizing value from their current vehicle.

- May seem skeptical or cautious.

    Strategy:

    - Be honest, transparent, and educational about the trade-in process.//
    - Show them how their current asset fits into the new opportunity.

The Reluctant Buyer
- Didn't plan to buy today.
- Often came in "just looking," feeling hesitant.

    Strategy:
    - Make them feel safe.
    - Ask open-ended questions to uncover hidden needs.
    - Create a low-pressure, inviting atmosphere.

Tip: Ask Open-Ended Discovery Questions

Questions like these open doors you can't find with scripts:

- *"What brings you in today?"*
- *"What's important to you in your next vehicle?"*

- "How do you see yourself using your car day-to-day?"

Each answer will guide you into understanding *who* they are not just *what* they want.

Accountability Challenge

Today, commit to intentionally identifying each customer's buyer type before you present a single vehicle.

Adjust your communication and offer based on *their needs*, not your agenda.

Reflection / Self-Assessment

- Did I take time to understand my buyer today before offering solutions?
- Which buyer types am I naturally more comfortable with? Which challenges me?
- How can I better tailor my approach tomorrow based on what I learned today?

Chapter 2
Listening is Selling

"The car is never the real product—trust is."

If there's one superpower that separates a mediocre salesperson from a legendary one, it's not slick talking, flashy charisma, or memorized specs, it's listening. Listening actively, intentionally, and with curiosity. Listening like their future, not your quota, depends on it.

The best salespeople don't start by showing off their product knowledge.
They start by mirroring their buyer's concerns, echoing their priorities, and becoming the person the customer feels truly heard by.

Before you talk features, talk about their needs.

Before you push a solution, pull out their story.

The Shift: The New Playbook for Automotive Sales Success

For decades, that stereotype has held, but today's market demands something radically different.
The customers have changed. They are smarter, more savvy, and have access to more information than ever before.
What they crave now isn't persuasion. It's partnership.

The shift starts with your paradigm, your mental model of what selling means.

Paradigm (noun): *A set of beliefs and assumptions that shape how we understand and approach a particular field.*

If you assume you already know everything about your buyer, you close your mind and often, you close the wrong deal.

If you stereotype or prejudge based on appearance, income level, or the first few words they say, you'll miss the real story driving their decisions.

The new paradigm?
You listen first.

You learn fast.
You lead later.

Listening doesn't mean waiting politely for your turn to talk. It means becoming a human mirror reflecting back concerns, priorities, and dreams the buyer may not even know how to articulate yet.

You don't assume you know the answers.
You discover them with patience, curiosity, and respect.

Every strong sale begins with a stronger ear.

Three-Step Process / Action Plan

Step 1: Practice Active Listening

- Be fully present. No mental checklists, no mental rush.

- Mirror their body language and emotional tone.

- Be attentive, nod, smile, show them you are truly tracking with them.

- Eye contact, but let your silence be a tool. Don't rush in to "save" awkward pauses.

Step 2: Use the Echo Technique

- Repeat part of what they say back to them in your own words.

- Example:
  Customer: *"I'm looking for something safer with all the new baby coming."*
  You: *"So having top-level safety features is going to be really important for your family's peace of mind."*

- Echoing shows understanding, not just hearing.

Step 3: Focus on Needs Before Features

- Don't launch into features or price right away.

- Stay in the "why" phase longer. Dig deeper:

    - *"Tell me more about what you're hoping to find today."*

    - *"What's most important for your next vehicle?"*

- Build the bridge between *their needs* and *your solution* later, not in the first 60 seconds.

Understanding the Buyer's Mind: The Psychology Behind the Purchase

Every customer standing in front of you carries more than a wish list, they carry motivations, fears, hopes, and concerns.

They are often shopping not for a car but for a solution to something happening in their life.

Income, motivations, family dynamics, career changes, personal victories, or even painful events often drive buying behavior far more than the features on a window sticker.

Your job:
Uncover the story behind the sale.
Become a student of human behavior, not just a product presenter.

Buyer Personality Quadrant Model: The Four Buying Personas

Here's a quick, practical framework for understanding buyer personalities you'll encounter based on decision speed and emotional vs. logical orientation.

Quadrant I:
The Visionary (Fast + Emotional)

Nickname: The Dream Buyer

- Impulsive, passionate, excited by experiences.

- Focused on feelings, status, style, and lifestyle enhancements.

Sales Strategy:

- Match their excitement.

- Paint a vivid picture of how this vehicle fits their dream.

- Avoid drowning them in specs or technical data — **sell the dream**.

Quadrant II:
The Analyst (Deliberate + Logical)

Nickname: The Researcher

- Methodical, detailed, cautious.
- Loves charts, comparisons, spreadsheets.

Sales Strategy:

- Provide data and logic clearly.
- Offer side-by-side analysis when possible.
- Don't rush. Their trust is earned through accuracy and respect.

Quadrant III:
The Guardian (Deliberate + Emotional)

Nickname: The Protector

- Focused on safety, reliability, long-term value.
- Family-first or security-minded.

Sales Strategy:
- Emphasize reliability, warranties, safety scores.
- Show empathy for their personal and family needs.
- Build trust slowly without pressure.

Quadrant IV:

The Driver (Fast + Logical)

Nickname: The Boss Buyer

- Time-conscious, direct, results-driven.
- ROI and efficiency focused.

Sales Strategy:
- Get to the point.
- Highlight value, performance, and quick payoff.
- Let them lead the conversation. Match their pace and professionalism.

Accountability Challenge

This week, practice active listening with every customer. Ask one question you normally wouldn't and stay silent long enough to hear the full answer.

Reflection / Self-Assessment

- What emotions might have been driving my last buyer's decision?
- Did I listen for needs or just react to questions?
- What could I have asked differently to understand their real motivation?

Your Maven Move: The Motivation Map

Choose a recent buyer you worked with. Without using surface answers like "they needed a car," map their real reason for purchase:

- What emotion may have driven their decision? (Fear, hope, excitement?)
- What deeper needs were they trying to meet?
- What could you ask next time to surface that need sooner?

Chapter 3

Presenting the Right Vehicle

"Because success isn't parked — it's driven."

If you want buyers to trust you, stop pushing products and start aligning solutions.

You're not just selling a car; you're matching a life to a vehicle that fits.

In a world flooded with options, the salesperson who wins isn't the one who talks the fastest, it's the one who listens the smartest.

The one who hears the need, sees the lifestyle, and points to the car that fits *them*, not just what's on sale.

Match the customer to the car. Don't push the car onto the customer.

Sell the story, not just the spec sheet.

The Corvette Story: Fitting the Customer, Not the Inventory

A friend of mine, who owned a local dealership, called me one afternoon, seemingly out of the blue.
He had just gotten in a special car: a white 40th Anniversary Edition Corvette. Mint condition. Low miles. The legendary LT1 engine under the hood.

He wasn't calling with a hard sell.
He wasn't pushing numbers or limited time offers.
He simply said, "It just fits you."

Now, here's the important part:
I had never once mentioned that I was looking for a Corvette. I wasn't.

But he knew something deeper — my history with Chevrolet, my appreciation for automotive craftsmanship, and my pride in ownership.

I agreed to come look at it.

After a little conversation and a casual walk around the lot, he said something that completely shifted my thinking, especially as a twenty-something year-old who hadn't yet thought about vehicles as investments.

"Drive it for a couple years," he said, "then return it."

Return it?

Not "sell it," not "get rid of it" — but "return it."

He explained that the Corvette would hold its value better than almost anything else I could buy at the time. If I enjoyed it for a few years, I could bring it back, trade it in, and lose very little compared to other vehicles.

I bought the car.
I drove it for three years, every mile, and was proud of the purchase.
When I finally (returned it)—traded it in, the depreciation was around $2,800 total, less than $1,000 per year of ownership.

Most cars would have lost four times that amount.

The lesson resonated with me forever, twofold:

Buying vehicles or any other larger items in life were assets or liabilities. The "return" mentioned above focused on ROI, (return on investment) which is the key to best align in the asset column. But part two the "return" was also psychologically offered as a sense of security, mindful of and ensuring the liability column stayed clean. When we align the two return factors into our sales process, we offer that insight and value life lesson value-add for our buyers. As we progress through this material, we will elaborate on further and continue to stay consistent to the use of the "Return" word.

When you match the right car to the right customer and frame the ownership story properly, you don't just sell a vehicle. You build lifelong trust.

Three-Step Process / Action Plan

Step 1: Align, Don't Push

- Start by understanding their lifestyle and values.
- Match their emotional needs first (safety, adventure, prestige, family).
- Only recommend vehicles that genuinely fit their needs, never force a fit.

Step 2: Use Real Stories to Build Credibility

- Share real experiences, your own or your customers', where the vehicle choice made a real difference.

- Be genuine. *Do not invent stories.* Authenticity is your greatest tool.

- Example: *"A customer of mine needed a safe commuter vehicle and ended up loving the reliability of the [Model X]. It fit their lifestyle perfectly."*

Step 3: Use Financial Smart Framing

- Show key statistics that prove smart investment:
    - Resale values
    - Reliability ratings
    - Warranty protections
- Frame ownership as **a smart decision**, not a risky one.
- Help the buyer visualize not just today's purchase but the smart, secure path for years to come.

The Power of the Word "Return": Influencing Buyer Confidence and Loyalty

Words matter in sales, more than you realize.

That one small change in language will radically reshape a customer's emotional experience of buying a car.

Instead of saying:

"You can always sell it or trade it in when you're ready."

Say:

"When you're ready, you can return it to us and we'll help you find your next perfect fit."

Why "Return" Works:

Reduced Buyer Anxiety:

- "Return" feels safer, like a guarantee.
- Reduces fear of making a bad decision, maintaining a clean liability column.

Increased Sense of Control:

- Buyers feel empowered, not trapped.
- They know they have options which reduces stress.

Subconscious Loyalty Cue:

- "Return" anchors your dealership as their future solution. This is the place the car eventually comes back to.
- They mentally associate you with easy transitions, not painful selling.

Preconditioning Repeat Business:

- "Return" plants the seed of coming back to you without effort. Reselling it or 'Trading in ' suggests they're on their own to find a place to trade it and your dealership risks losing them to a competitor.

- Sets you up as their natural long-term partner— a revolving door sales approach.

How to Use "Return" in Conversation:

Instead of:

"You can sell or trade it when you're ready."

Say:

"Down the road, when your needs change, you can return it to us and we'll make the next step just as easy."

Instead of:

"You can get rid of it if it doesn't work."

Say:

"If your lifestyle changes, we're here to help you return it and upgrade to the next chapter of your journey."

Framing the purchase this way builds trust, lowers resistance, and strengthens loyalty before the paperwork is even signed.

Beyond the Lot: Standing Out, Selling Smart, and Building Loyalty for Life

Winning the sale is only the beginning.

To become a true Maven Maker, someone buyers talk about, refer, and return to, you must **own every part of the customer experience**.

Here's what lasting success looks like beyond the car lot:

Trait	Application
First Impressions	Dress, speak, and carry yourself with warmth and authority.
Posture and Body Language	Show energy and approachability, not arrogance or detachment.
Charisma	Be relatable but commanding. Confidence invites trust.
Attentiveness	Listen with care — remember names, kids, hobbies. Make people feel seen.
Responsibility	Always do what you say you will. Every promise fulfilled cements loyalty.

People don't just buy cars; they buy people they trust.

Hearing What Isn't Said

Melissa had only been selling cars for a year, but she had a gift that couldn't be taught, she listened with her whole heart.

One afternoon, a couple walked into her dealership: Mark and Denise.

Mark was animated, excited, the perfect "dream customer," or so it seemed.

But Melissa noticed something else.

Denise, Mark's wife, said almost nothing.
When they sat inside one of the sedans, Denise didn't even touch the door handle; she simply stared quietly out the window.

Melissa could've charged ahead, demoing horsepower and sport packages for Mark.
But she paused.

She turned to Denise and asked gently:
"I want to make sure we get something you'll both love. What matters most to you when you're driving every day?"

It was like a dam breaking.

Denise opened up about cramped school runs, about long drives with kids, about wanting space, comfort, and peace on the road.

Mark's tone shifted too.
He listened. He reconsidered.

They test drove a midsize crossover and bought it the same day.

Later, Denise pulled Melissa aside and said:
"You were the first person who made me feel like I had a say. Thank you."

Accountability Challenge

This week, during every customer interaction, pause intentionally to invite the quieter voice into the conversation.

Use the line:
"What's important to you in this decision?"
Then — just listen.

Reflection / Self-Assessment

- Am I paying attention to what's unsaid during my sales conversations?

- How often do I notice body language and silent signals?

- How could I create more space for hidden needs to surface?

Chapter 4
Finding the Buyers

"In the first five minutes, you're not selling a car, you're selling comfort."

You can have the best cars, the best lot, the best ads but if you aren't meeting people where they are, you're missing your next buyer.
 Finding new customers isn't about waiting, it's about walking, talking, and inviting trust.

Sales aren't found behind a desk. They're found out in the world.

Every day offers one new opportunity if you're willing to look for it.

The Maven Maker Approach: Turning Buyers into Believers

The best salespeople don't just sit and wait for "ups" to stroll through the lot.
They create new opportunities by connecting, listening, and becoming part of the community.

Imagine building a career where:

- People recognize your face before they recognize your logo.

- Your name comes up at community events without you even being there.

- Your customers introduce you to their friends without hesitation.

That kind of influence isn't built by accident.

It's built one conversation at a time.

The Salesperson's Marketing Plan: Finding New Buyers One Person at a Time

I. Where to Find Potential Buyers Outside the Dealership

1. Local Businesses and Networking Groups

- Visit real estate offices, contractor meetups, and medical sales teams, industries where transportation matters.

- Attend charity events, Chamber of Commerce mixers or sponsor small events.

- Show up at trade shows or job fairs, be the only car expert in the room.

2. Community Involvement

- Sponsor a youth sports team, get your name on jerseys or banners.

- Volunteer, give back through charity events, arrive in a dealership vehicle, proudly branded.

- Be present at school fundraisers, PTA nights, and parent gatherings.

3. Lifestyle-Based Locations

- Coffee shops, gyms, golf courses, dog parks, not to pitch, but to build relationships.

- A friendly conversation today can become a sale six months from now.

II. Social Strategy & Referrals

1. Facebook Groups and Marketplace

- Join local buy/sell groups, offer advice, not just ads.

- Post content like: *"5 Tips for Choosing Your Next Family SUV"* instead of shouting about discounts.

2. Instagram and TikTok Reels

- Short, fun videos:

- - "What $400/month gets you today."
  - "Best cars for new grads."
  - "This week only"

3. Referral Rewards

- Offer small gifts: $50 gas cards, free oil change for every referral.
- Keep it simple:
  "Know someone looking? Text me their name. I'll treat them like family."

III. Daily Practice: The "Just One More" Method

Mission: Talk to one new prospect every day — outside the dealership.

How:

- Start each day asking: *"Where can I meet one new potential buyer today?"*
- Visit local restaurants, community events, and small businesses.
- Always carry a "mini card" with your name, text info, and 3 reasons to call you.

Mini Card Example:
"Need a new car? Save $40/mo. Ask me how!"

Track It:

- Create a calendar or whiteboard.
- Write the name or location of every new prospect you meet.
- Set a reminder to follow up.

IV. Bonus: Power of "Thank You" Marketing

- Send handwritten thank-you cards after every customer visit, test drive, or referral.
- Include two extra business cards inside each envelope.
- Personalize the message:
  "Thanks for your time today. Let's find the perfect fit when you're ready. I'm just a text away!"

Relationships outlast inventory. Always.

The Maven Maker Plan: Standing Apart and Adding Real Value

I. Stand-Apart Strategy: Deliver the Experience, Not Just the Car

1. Pre-Visit Touchpoint

- Send a short, personalized video before their appointment:
  "Hi [Name], I'm [Your Name], I can't wait to meet you. I already have a few great options in mind based on what you shared!"

2. Curated Appointment

- Have a small welcome sign at your desk.
- Offer water or coffee immediately.
- Prepare a comparison sheet even if they only asked about one car.

3. Story-Based Selling

- Share authentic success stories:
  "Sarah found the perfect fit for her growing family last month, let's find yours too."

II. Value-Add Touchpoints

1. Personalized Test Drive Route

- Plan the drive to reflect their real life, school runs, freeway merging, tight parking.

2. Ownership Ready Kit

- New Owner Welcome Bag:
  - Tire pressure gauge

- Car wash voucher
- Key tag with their name
- QR code linking to your contact info, dealership review page, and service scheduler.

3. 30-Day Follow-Up

- Call with no agenda:
  "How's the car treating you? Need help with anything?"

This small gesture cements loyalty forever.

III. Referral Engine: Make It Easy to Rave About You

1. Car Coach Identity

- Introduce yourself not as a "salesperson," but a Car Coach:
  "I'm here to help you."

2. Post-Sale Referral Message

- Text after delivery:
  "Loved helping you today! Thank you."

3. Social Shoutouts

- With permission, post a Delivery Day photo and tag them on social media to ensure it hits their page:
"*Another smart buyer on the road! Congrats [Name]!*"

IV. Maven Moments: Experiences That Create Stories

- Send a birthday card.
- Send a thank-you note featuring them and a photo of their car. Repost social media pictures on anniversary and tag them again. A reason to reach out again.
- Invitations to dealer events.
- Host quarterly "VIP Car Clinics" to teach basic car care. Meet and greet other enthusiasts.

Recognition Wall:

Start a "Happy Drivers" wall, digital loop feed on TV in the dealership and on social media showcasing happy customers and dealer events.

Buyers talk when they feel seen, valued, and remembered.

V. Result: The Maven Effect

Buyers talk when:

- They feel truly known.
- You did what others forgot.
- You followed up without an agenda.
- You made buying a car feel easy, smart, and joyful.

Mavens refer because you gave them something rare:
A buying experience worth sharing.

Rule of Thumb:
"If they trust you, they'll come back, even if it's years later."

The First Five Minutes

The first five minutes with a customer decide everything.

Get it wrong, and no amount of inventory or pricing can fix it.
Get it right, and they'll want to stay, listen, and buy.

The Day You Lose or Win

Mike was the kind of guy who looked like he had it all figured out — pressed shirts, knowledgeable, fast talking.

But Mike moved too fast.

One morning, a young couple arrived at the lot, stroller in tow, exhaustion written on their faces.

Mike approached confidently:
Looking to upgrade that SUV?"
He rattled off models, payments, trade values.
All within five minutes.

They nodded politely and left just as politely.

Later that day, Kim, another salesperson, spotted the same couple lingering in the parking lot.

Instead of diving in, Kim smiled, complimented their baby, and said simply:
"Let's just walk and talk. You lead the way."

They chatted. They strolled.
 Kim didn't pitch once.

Two days later, they came back and bought a new family SUV from Kim. Mike hadn't "read the room" — the personality quadrant overlooked.

Accountability Challenge

For the next three customers, focus the first five minutes on connection, not presentation.

Use this line:
"Welcome! I'm glad you're here. Want to walk and talk or just look around first?"

Watch how it shifts their posture, their guard, and their willingness to stay.

Reflection / Self-Assessment

- Did I match their energy — or force my own?
- Did I invite conversation — or push information?
- Did they feel seen — or sold to?

Chapter 5
Overcoming Objections

"People don't buy the drive—they buy how it makes them feel."

Objections are not obstacles — they're opportunities. They're a buyer's way of saying: "I'm interested, but I need more reassurance."

When handled correctly, objections become bridges to deeper trust, not roadblocks to the sale.

Listen, acknowledge, and assist, don't argue.

Every "no" you hear is really just a "not yet" — if you handle it with care.

Objection Handling: The Art of Empathy and Expertise

Every buyer hesitates at some point.

It's not because they don't want to buy — it's because they're scared of buying wrong.

- Fear of overpaying.

- Fear of being rushed.
- Fear of missing a better deal.

The best sales professionals don't bulldoze through these fears, they walk alongside the buyer, guiding them toward clarity without pressure.

Handling objections is about three things:

1. Acknowledging their concern with empathy.
2. Asking a deeper question to understand the real issue.
3. Assisting them by offering clarity, not control.

One powerful tool to use is the 3 F's Technique:

- **Feel:** *"I understand how you feel..."*
- **Felt:** *"Others have felt the same way..."*
- **Found:** *"What they found was..."*

It's not manipulation, it's making the buyer feel heard, understood, and supported in their decision.

Common Objections and Rebuttals (With Empathy)

1. "I need to think about it."

Rebuttal:
"I completely understand, this is a big decision. While you're considering it, may I ask: is there a specific concern I can help clear up? Sometimes having the right information makes thinking easier."

2. "I'm just looking."

Rebuttal:
"Perfect, that's how most of our customers start. While you're looking, would it help if I just showed you a few options that fit what you're interested in? No pressure, just good information."

3. "I saw it cheaper online."

Rebuttal:
"That's fair, online prices can vary a lot based on what's included. I can help you compare if you wish. The one you're

looking at here might have better warranty coverage, service history, or inspection standards. Want to review what's included together?"

---

4. "I don't want to be rushed."

Rebuttal:

"Completely understand, I wouldn't want you to feel rushed either. I'm here if you have questions or need anything."

---

5. "I need to talk to my spouse/partner first."

Rebuttal:

"Absolutely. Would it help if we pulled together a few details you can show them? Or we can set a time for you both to test drive it again together."

---

6. "I'm not ready to buy today."

Rebuttal:

"No problem at all. You don't have to buy for us to offer great advice. Here are a few options so when you are ready, you feel 100% confident."

7. "I want to shop around first."

Rebuttal:

"Smart move. If you'd like, I can even help you create a checklist to compare while you shop. Whether you buy here or elsewhere, I want you to make the right decision."

---

8. "The payments are too high."

Rebuttal:

"Thanks for sharing that—that's important. Let's explore a few adjustments. A small change in term or down payment can sometimes make a big difference. Would you like to see a few options?"

---

9. "Can you do better on the price?"

Rebuttal:

"I hear you—you want the best value possible. Let me check comps and double-check with my manager. Do you feel we are overpriced? Based on? In the meantime, what price would make this a no-brainer for you, and why?"

10. "I'm not sure if I should lease or finance."

Rebuttal:

"Great question! Leasing and financing each have perks. Leasing gives you lower payments and new cars more often; financing builds ownership. Let's take two minutes to look at both side-by-side." And consider the "Return" future values and potential tax savings or write off.

The Emotional Power of the Test Drive

Tasha understood something many salespeople miss: The test drive isn't about showing off the car, it's about inviting the buyer to live inside a new future.

Before every drive, she'd ask a simple, powerful question:
"What's the first trip you'd take in this?"

Some said "work."
Some smiled and said, "weekend getaway."
One man's voice softened when he said, *"I'd pick my daughter up from college."*

During the drive, Tasha let the moments breathe.

- She stayed quiet when needed.
- She pointed things out only when customers noticed them first.
- She let the customer *feel* the fit not just *hear* about it.

The result?

Her buyers didn't just buy cars.
They bought a feeling.
They bought trust.

And when they drove off the lot, they weren't just leaving with a new car, they were leaving with a story.

Accountability Challenge

During your next objection or hesitation, be sure to apply the 3 F's Technique — Feel, Felt, Found
Practice transforming objections into conversations, not conflicts.

Reflection / Self-Assessment

- When I hear an objection, do I react defensively or lean into understanding?
- Am I offering clarity or pushing solutions too fast?
- How could I slow down and build trust during critical moments of hesitation?

Your Maven Move: "The Emotional Drive"

Before your next test drive:

- Ask: *"What kind of day are you hoping this car makes easier?"*
- Ask: *"Who's usually riding with you?"*
- Ask: *"Where would this car take you first?"*

Then listen quietly as they imagine.

Post-drive, ask: *"What stood out to you?"* and watch what feelings surface.

Chapter 6
Closing with Confidence

"An objection isn't an obstacle — it's an invitation to prove your worth."

Closing a deal is about trust, timing, and respectful partnership.

You should only move toward the close after the buyer feels heard, understood, and valued.

Ask for the sale when it's a natural next step, not a forced finish.

Present choices, not ultimatums.

Protect your reputation because your story will be shared with many.

Hearing the Customer, Not Hurting the Relationship

Customers aren't just buying a car; they're buying an experience.

And experiences get talked about.

A positive buying experience might get mentioned once or twice.

A negative buying experience? It gets repeated ten times over or more.

I know this firsthand. I'm still telling both sides and now using these encounters in this course material. Can you imagine the depth of reach for each? Which side do you want to represent?

What Not to Do: The Burberry Tie Deal

Years ago, I walked into a Chicagoland dealership, ready to buy. This dealership didn't negotiate on listed sale prices. But trade in valuations were on another level of negotiation tactics!

I had everything lined up:

- The exact car I wanted. (My wife wanted)
- A fair value for my trade-in.
- A reasonable offer based on real market research.

But after hours of frustrating negotiations on my trade, the salesperson continued to lowball and wasted my time with games. Still up selling his new car— which I was already committing to buy.

Eventually, I had enough.

"I'm done," I said. *"You've wasted my time."*

Cue the theatrics.

The manager arrived, offering "last-minute deals", desperate plays designed to sound like compromises but lacking any real sincerity.

Meanwhile, the salesperson who clearly thought highly of himself filled the awkward silences talking about his new Burberry tie, a "gift from his wife."
He prattled on about how sharp he looked while I simply waited to get my keys back.

Just when I was ready to walk out, he pulled the oldest trick in the book:
A fake phone call from the manager with a "miraculous" last-second deal.

I cut him off.
"We're done talking."

I left, furious and disappointed.

But it wasn't over.

On my cold, dark winter drive home, the calls started:

- We are really close to your number.
- Him insisting he had now "gotten the numbers closer right." Working for me.
- Him begging to "make it right."
- Six calls later. Each letting him know my mile marker getting closer to home. His time was running out.

Finally, I told him:
"I gave you my final number for the trade. If there's no deal by the time I get home, I'm blocking your calls."

I pulled into my driveway and sure enough, the phone rang again.
He promised everything I had asked for and more. He claimed to have everything now exactly as I wanted—after his gamesmanship.
He even offered to deliver the car to my house since I was unwilling to return even at my negotiating number.

My wife wanted the car so after discussions with her, I agreed, but with a new demand:
"My price hasn't changed. I'll return and do the deal. But now, I want the Burberry tie."

He laughed... I didn't.

There was silence… and then resignation.

When I arrived to sign the papers, I didn't sit down. I walked straight up to him, reached out, took the tie, crumpled it into my pocket and then, and only then, signed the paperwork.

I never returned to that dealership.

Lesson:
Confidence in closing isn't about theatrics, manipulation, or wearing fancy ties.
It's about respect, timing, and building trust that lasts beyond the sale.

Confidence Line to Remember:

"Let's find a solution that fits perfectly; your needs, your budget, and your timeline."

Calm.
Professional.
Customer-centered.

Three-Step Process / Action Plan

Step 1: Ask for the Sale Naturally

- Use invitation language, not pressure language: *"Would you like to see what the monthly would look like?"*

- It feels cooperative, not combative.

Step 2: Offer Choices, Not Ultimatums

- Always present two or three options:

  "We can structure it this way, or if you'd prefer, we could extend the term to lower your monthly."

- Options empower the customer. Ultimatums repel them.

Step 3: Respect Their Time and Story

- Move at their pace, especially at the close.

- Finish with the same warmth you started with.

- Remember: You're not just closing a sale — you're opening the door for future business.

Leave them with a story they'll tell proudly not as a cautionary tale. Remember the negative story has longer legs.

The Price Struggle Turned Into Trust

Jonah, a seasoned salesperson, faced a familiar situation: A couple, Susan and David, had found the perfect car but hesitated at the price.

Susan said, "It's just a little more than we planned to spend."

Instead of defending the price or rushing into discounts, Jonah paused.
He smiled and asked,
"I hear you, budgets matter. What's the most important feature for you in this purchase?"

Susan responded immediately:
"Safety and space. We have two kids and we're thinking about growing the family."

Jonah didn't argue.
He aligned:
"Got it. Let's take a minute to see how this model actually saves you money long-term and protects what matters most to you."

He showed them:

- Warranty value.
- Resale strength.
- Cost savings on maintenance.

Susan and David didn't just leave with a car, they left feeling smart, respected, and protected.

They bought because Jonah turned their hesitation into a conversation not a confrontation.

Accountability Challenge

During your next sales conversation, when you sense hesitation: Identify the problem. Offer the solution.

- Pause.
- Ask a soft, open-ended question about their priority.
- Offer options, not pressure.

Turn hesitation into a doorway, not a dead end.

Reflection / Self-Assessment

- When I hear "no" or "not yet," do I get defensive or curious?

- Am I offering real solutions or just pushing my agenda?

- How could I close conversations with more dignity and collaboration?

Your Maven Move: "The Objection Partnership"

During your next objection:

- **Listen:** Acknowledge what they're feeling.

- **Clarify:** Ask what's really driving the concern.

- **Collaborate:** Present new ways to meet their needs without forcing anything.

You're not overcoming them, you're overcoming fear, together.

Chapter 7
Becoming a Lifetime Advisor

"A confident close is an invitation to make the right choice, not a push for a decision."

Your real goal in automotive sales isn't to close a deal today, it's to earn a buyer for life. You're not just a salesperson; you're an automotive advisor building a personal brand. Since my early years in the automotive world, I've spent the past three decades plus in business. The same community and serving many of the same faces. I built a lasting reputation.

Think beyond this sale. Think lifetime trust.

When they think of buying, trading, or referring to a car, your name should be the first they say: "Call my guy."

Becoming "Their Car Person". The One They Always Think Of

As of early 2025, the average transaction price for a new vehicle in the U.S. sits around $49,740 with full-size trucks reaching over $64,000, and EVs averaging $55,544.

Buying a car today isn't a small decision, it's often the second largest purchase a family makes, right after buying a home.

- New car buyers have an average household income of about $115,000.
- Used car buyers average $96,000.
- Electric vehicle buyers are even higher, at $140,000.

Meanwhile, the cost of owning a car has risen sharply, now about $12,182 per year.

This means buyers are more selective, more cautious, and more value-focused than ever before.

They want someone they trust to guide them, not sell to them.

When you position yourself as an advisor:

- You become their automatic go-to.
- You bypass price wars.

- You build long-term relationships that drive recurring revenue, not just one-off commissions.

The "One More" Strategy

It doesn't require fancy algorithms or giant advertising budgets.

Make a commitment, start with one simple idea:
Find and reach just one more connection every week.

Out-of-the-Box Ways to Find "One More":

- Attend a local event (not as a vendor, as a human).
- Join a community Facebook group and answer a car question.
- Host a coffee meetup for first-time buyers.
- Send a "Car Care Tip of the Month" email to past customers.
- Drop off thank-you treats to businesses near your dealership.
- Post a short video: *"Three smart questions to ask before buying your next car."*

Personal Brand and Growth Strategy: Plant one seed a day, water it, and watch your network.

What This Chapter Teaches:

- Closing isn't pushing, it's finding alignment between their needs and your solution.
- Great closers listen more than they speak during final moments.
- Confidence in the close comes from clarifying the buyer's wants, not from forcing the paperwork.

Three-Step Process / Action Plan

Step 1: Position Yourself as Their Advisor

- Shift your mindset: You're advising, not selling.
- Speak like a trusted guide:
  "Let's find what fits your needs, budget, and timeline perfectly."

Step 2: Ask Empowering Closing Questions

- "What's the first thing you'd do with your new car?"

- *"Can I get everything lined up so we can make it official today?"*

- *"What's the best way to make this work for you?"*

These questions invite action without pressure.

Step 3: Let Silence Be Your Superpower

- After asking, pause.

- Let them process.

- Confidence isn't just in speaking; it's in allowing space for decisions.

Accountability Challenge

Next time you feel the closing moment approaching:

- Pause and ask an empowering question.

- Resist the urge to talk over their silence.

- Watch how much easier the "yes" becomes when the buyer feels fully in control.

Reflection / Self-Assessment

- Am I confident enough to ask for the sale — or do I hesitate?

- Do I close with pressure — or with partnership?

- How could I make the closing experience feel better for my buyer — and for myself?

Your Maven Move: "The Confident Close"

Before you ask for the close:

- Ask about their first adventure in the car.

- Ask how this purchase fits their life — not just their payment schedule.

- Lead with life, then close with logic.

Buyers will remember the confidence you gave them far longer than the contract they signed.

Chapter 8
Building a Business Inside the Business

"The sale doesn't end with paperwork; it begins with the relationship."

Grow a personal brand that drives consistent traffic, referrals, and repeat buyers.

Your dealership is your platform, but your name is the real business you're building.

Every positive experience creates a customer for life and every lifetime customer becomes your best "free' Maven-marketing.

The Power of the Personal Follow-Up

Danny had been selling cars for a while, but like many salespeople, once the paperwork was signed, his attention shifted back to the next buyer.

One day, while walking through the dealership, he paused.

He realized he hadn't checked in with Martin, a customer he sold a family sedan to six months earlier.

Danny remembered something his mentor, Greg, had once said:

"Sales don't end with the paperwork. They end with the relationship."

That day, Danny picked up the phone.

He wasn't calling to upsell.
He wasn't calling to pitch a service package.
He simply called to check in.

Danny:
"Hey Martin, it's Danny from the dealership. Just wanted to check in and see how things are going with your new car. Still meeting your needs?"

Martin:
"Wow, thanks for calling, Danny. Actually, it's been great. I had a minor issue with the AC last week, but they fixed it no problem."

Danny:
 "Glad to hear it was handled! And if you ever need anything

else — questions, service tips, even advice on accessories — I'm here for you anytime."

Martin:
"I really appreciate that. Actually, I've been telling my brother about you — he's thinking about upgrading his car soon."

That simple, thoughtful call turned into a referral — and another sale.

More importantly, it planted a seed of loyalty that would grow stronger with time.

What This Chapter Teaches:

- Sales don't stop after the signature — they start with relationship building.

- Genuine follow-up creates trust, referrals, and long-term success.

- A thoughtful check-in outlasts any slick sales pitch.

Customers remember who cared about them after the deal was done.

Building a Business Inside the Business

When you think like a lifetime advisor, not just a salesperson, you create your own personal brand inside the dealership.

It doesn't matter how strong the economy is.
It doesn't matter if inventory is tight, or incentives are thin.

Your brand is your security.

Here's how to build it:

Personal Brand Growth Strategies:

- Follow Up Thoughtfully: Reach out not to sell, but to support.

- Deliver Value Without Expectation: Share service tips, maintenance reminders, and check-in texts.

- Make It Personal: Remember their kids' names, their pets, their hobbies.

- Stay Visible: Post helpful content on social media (not just inventory).

- Ask for Referrals the Right Way: Position it as helping their friends, not helping your paycheck.

You're building a business where trust is the currency and experience is the brand.

The Follow-Up: Keeping the Relationship Alive

Follow-up isn't annoying when it's done right.
It's comforting.
It's respectful.
It says: *"You matter beyond the sale."*

Follow-Up Timeline Example:

> **1 Week After the Sale:**
> *"Hi [Customer], just checking in, are you still happy with your new car? Let me know if you have any questions!"*
>
> Focus: Immediate reassurance, open-door feeling.
>
> **1 Month After the Sale:**
> *"Hope you're loving the car! If you ever need service tips, upgrade advice, or anything else, just reach out. I'm here for you."*
>
> Focus: Service positioning, gentle long-term connection.

6 Months After the Sale:

"Hi [Customer], just wanted to say thanks again for choosing us. How's everything going? Still love the drive?"

Focus: Relationship nurture, genuine touchpoint.

Challenge: The Thoughtful Check-In

For the next two weeks:

Set a personal goal:
Make at least one thoughtful follow-up call, text, or email per day.

Track how many:

- Positive responses you get.
- Referrals you generate.
- Repeat conversations you open.

Small actions, multiplied daily, create massive momentum.

Accountability Challenge

Create a follow-up plan for your last 10 customers:

- 1 Week check-in
- 1 Month support text
- 6 Month appreciation message

Stick to it and watch your referrals grow.

Reflection / Self-Assessment

- What if I cared? When was the last time I followed up with no agenda. Just care.
- Am I building relationships or just closing transactions?
- How can I make my customers feel supported long after they drive away?

Your Maven Move: "The Thoughtful Check-In"

Remember:

The customer may forget the specs you rattled off.

They may forget the sticker price.

But they'll never forget the way you made them feel after they drove away.

They'll never forget the first person who called just to say thank you.

Chapter 9
Creating Enthusiastic Fans
(Not Just Customers)

"The best form of advertising is a happy customer who is eager to share their experience."

Want a marketing budget you don't have to pay for? Create maven fans.

When you deliver more than a sale, when you deliver an experience, your customers will do your advertising for you.

Referrals don't come from satisfied buyers, they come from delighted ones.

Turn every buyer into a believer and every believer into a walking billboard for your name.

The Power of a Referral: How One Sale Became Two

Carlos had been working at the dealership for just over a year.

He had learned how to close deals.
He had learned how to keep customers happy.

But what he hadn't yet learned was the power of a great referral.

That changed when he met Eliza.

Eliza came into the dealership looking for a new SUV. She wasn't just shopping; she had a mission.

Her friend, Vanessa, had bought from Carlos a few months earlier and raved about the experience.
Thanks to Vanessa's glowing recommendation, Eliza's expectations were high.

Carlos delivered.

He listened carefully, guided her patiently, and ensured the buying process was smooth, transparent, and fun.

Two weeks after Eliza drove off in her new SUV, Carlos picked up the phone and made a simple check-in call.

Carlos:
"Hey Eliza, just checking in, how's everything going with your new car?"

Eliza:

"It's been perfect — thank you so much! Actually, my best friend Miranda is thinking about buying soon too."

Carlos:

"That's fantastic! I'd love to offer Miranda the same experience. I really appreciate you — and I'd be honored to help her too."

Two months later, Miranda walked into the dealership and another deal was closed.

More importantly, Carlos had learned a powerful truth: One great customer experience multiplies itself — if you nurture it.

What This Chapter Teaches:

- Referrals aren't automatic — they're earned.
- Deliver an exceptional experience first.
- Then proactively create opportunities for your customers to spread the word.

Referrals flow naturally when trust is real, and care is felt.

Turning Referrals Into Revenue

Referrals are the secret weapon of every high-performing salesperson. They create a pipeline of ready, trusting buyers, buyers who already believe in you before they ever meet you.

But it doesn't happen by chance.

You must ask intentionally.
You must follow up thoughtfully.
You must over-deliver consistently.

How to Build a Referral System

1. Deliver Legendary Service First

No one refers to average experiences.
They only refer to moments that stand out.

Every interaction matters:

- Your first hello.
- Your patience on the test drive.

- Your excitement at delivery day.
- Your thoughtful follow-up calls.

One way or another, they are going to share their experience. Give them a positive story they can't wait to share.

2. Ask for Referrals the Right Way

One Week After the Sale:
"Hi [Customer], just wanted to check in and see how you're loving your new car. If you have any friends or family thinking about buying, I'd love the opportunity to help them."

One Month After the Sale:
"Hope everything's going great! Just a reminder, if anyone you know could use a little car-buying help, I'm here. I promise to take excellent care of them — just like I did for you."

Keep it casual.
Keep it customer-centered.

3. Track Your Progress

Set a monthly referral goal:

"I will generate at least 3 referrals this month."

Track weekly:

- How many follow-up touches you made.
- How many referral conversations you started.
- How many actual referrals came through.

Visibility drives focus and focus drives results.

4. Create a Simple Referral Rewards Program

Offer something meaningful:

- A $50 gas card.
- A free oil change.
- A personalized thank-you gift.

Let customers know you appreciate their referrals not because it's a transaction, but because it's trust extended.

5. Celebrate Referrers Publicly

With permission, thank them:

- Tag them on social media.
- Send a handwritten note.
- Call them personally to say thank you.

Recognition deepens loyalty.

Accountability Action Plan

Action	Goal
Referral Goal	3+ referrals per month
Follow-Up Strategy	1-week, 1-month, 6-month touchpoints
Track Conversations	Log each referral conversation and outcome
Celebrate Referrers	Handwritten notes, small gifts, public thanks
Weekly Review	Adjust strategies based on results

Consistency compounds success.

Accountability Challenge

For the next two weeks:

During every post-sale follow-up, ask for a referral.
Track your asks and any new referrals generated.
Celebrate each one no matter how small.

Reflection / Self-Assessment

- Do I intentionally ask for referrals or leave it to chance?

- It's on you! Am I really creating such a great experience that customers *want* to refer me?

- How could I strengthen my referral follow-up and recognition strategy?

Your Maven Move: "The Referral-Focused Follow-Up"

Treat every customer not just as a transaction — but as a future ambassador.
Their satisfaction today is your pipeline for tomorrow.

A happy customer tells a few people.
A raving fan tells everyone.

Chapter 10

Leveraging Technology for Sales Success

"Technology is a tool that should empower you to do what you do best, connect with people."

Technology won't replace great salespeople.
It will empower the best ones to serve more buyers, more efficiently, and more personally.

Think of technology as your backstage personal assistant not your replacement.

When used correctly, digital tools give you more time, better timing, and smarter touches all while keeping your human connection front and center.

Embracing Technology for Greater Efficiency

Jenna had been selling cars for over five years.
She was good at it, trusted by her customers, respected by her team.

But when it came to technology, Jenna was hesitant.

- She preferred handwritten notes.
- She liked face-to-face conversations.
- She didn't trust the idea of "apps doing the work."

Then, her manager introduced her to a Customer Relationship Management (CRM) system.

Reluctantly, Jenna tried it.
And everything changed.

With the CRM:

- She tracked every customer conversation.
- She set personalized follow-up reminders.
- She knew when customers were due for service, lease renewals, or vehicle upgrades.

Using her dealership's app:

- She sent custom offers based on each customer's preferences.
- She stayed visible and helpful without feeling intrusive.

One day, Jenna got an automatic alert:
A past customer had booked a service appointment.

Jenna remembered their earlier conversations about wanting an upgrade "someday."
She reached out through the app and within a week, she had closed a new deal.

No cold calls.
No hard sales.
Just the right message, at the right time, with the right heart.

What This Chapter Teaches:

- Technology doesn't replace personal connections, it amplifies it.
- CRM systems, apps, and marketing automation help you stay organized and relevant.
- Using technology intelligently frees you to spend more time where it matters, with people.

The future of car sales belongs to those who combine heart and tech.

The Team Maven Model

Technology helps individuals scale.
But emotional intelligence helps teams scale.

At its core, The Team Maven Model is about training, tracking, and motivating a team that lives the Maven mindset:

- Serve first.
- Sell second.
- Build trust always.

The Shift That Changed It All

Jacob had been at the dealership for three months.
He was doing everything "by the book" —

- Quoting financing options.
- Upselling warranties.
- Listing specs like a walking brochure.

His numbers? Fine.
His customer loyalty? Good enough.

Then Linda walked onto the lot.

Linda was a recently widowed retired teacher.
She wasn't shopping for horsepower or heated seats.
She was shopping for peace of mind.

And for the first time, Jacob changed his approach.

He asked better questions:

- *"What's important to you when you drive?"*
- *"How do you want to feel behind the wheel?"*
- *"What did you love most about your last car?"*

He listened beyond the answers.
He heard the story behind the specs.

Instead of pushing the highest-margin car, he found the right car.

Three days later, Linda brought cookies to thank him.
A week later, her son bought his car from Jacob too.
Six months later, two of her church friends became customers as well.

Jacob learned:
"When you sell a car, you make a commission.
When you serve a human, you build a movement."

What This Chapter Teaches:

- Every buyer is a person first, a customer second.
- Trust outperforms technique every time.
- Your biggest wins aren't your biggest sales, they're your biggest relationships.

When you slow down to hear what's really needed, you speed up everything that matters.

Reflection: Step Into Their World

Emotional Intelligence (EQ) isn't just a buzzword. It's a superpower for modern sales professionals.

High-EQ salespeople:

- Recognize emotional drivers behind decisions.
- Adjust based on subtle cues.

- Connect in ways that no script or closing tactic can replicate.

5 Key Components of Emotional Intelligence in Sales

1. Self-Awareness: Understand your own emotions, triggers, and communication tendencies.

   Sales impact: Stay calm under pressure. Recognize when to slow down.

2. Self-Regulation: Think before reacting. Stay poised.

   Sales impact: You don't panic at objections; you pivot with patience.

3. Motivation: Stay driven even when results are slow.

   Sales impact: You bounce back quickly from rejections and stay optimistic for the next opportunity.

4. Empathy: See the sale through their eyes.

Sales impact: You ask better questions, read body language, and meet real needs — not imagined ones.

5. Social Skills: Build authentic rapport. Handle conversations smoothly.

   Sales impact: You close more deals — not because you're slick, but because you're sincere.

Using EQ to Build Relationships

Reading Cues: Notice whether buyers need more data or more emotional reassurance.

Building Trust: Be present. Let them feel heard. Mirror their pace and energy.

Handling Objections Gracefully: See past the words and recognize the emotion underneath.

Your Maven Move: "The Next Buyer" Practice

Exercise:

Visualize your next buyer walking onto the lot. They may not know exactly what they need — but they know how they want to feel.

Before they say a word, ask yourself:

- *What might they be feeling before they walk in?*
- *What might they be afraid of?*
- *What would make this interaction unforgettable in the best way?*
- *What's one better question I could ask today that I've never asked before?*

Then go use it.

Watch what changes.

Accountability Action Plan

Action	Goal
Technology Adoption	Implement 1 new tool in 10 days (CRM, social, or email platform)
EQ Practice	Ask 1 deeper connection question per customer
Follow-Up Improvement	Track every customer's touchpoints using tech
Referral Growth	Tie digital touchpoints to human gratitude

Track results monthly.

Celebrate small wins, they lead to big ones.

Reflection / Self-Assessment

- Am I using technology as a tool or as a crutch?

- Am I connecting with people or just contacting them?

- How can I combine tech and heart more intentionally moving forward?

Chapter 11
Building Your Personal Brand as a Sales Professional

"Your personal brand is the story you tell the world. Make it a story worth telling."

In today's world, buyers aren't just shopping for cars, they're shopping for people they trust.
They want a guide, an expert, a recognizable face who stands out from the crowd.

Your personal brand is your secret weapon.
It's what makes buyers choose you and remember you.

If you don't build your brand intentionally, others will define it for you or forget you altogether.

The Power of Personal Branding

Tom had been a car salesperson for a few years.
He was competent. Reliable.
But he felt invisible.

He blended into the crowd of other salespeople, lacking any standout identity or reputation.

One day, his manager pulled him aside and gave him a piece of advice that changed everything:

Manager:
"Tom, if you want to stand out, you need a personal brand — a differential that sets you apart from any other salesperson.
Think about how you want people to perceive you — and why they'd specifically ask for you."

Tom went home and thought hard. Differential?
What did he love most about his job?
What excited him?

The answer was clear: performance cars.

He decided to make that his brand. A Super Car expert.

Tom became the expert, not just of his dealership but in the community. Word spread quickly.

He took small but consistent steps:

- Posting videos about performance models on social media.
- Writing quick articles explaining horsepower, torque, and handling.

- Hosting Saturday "Performance Test Drive Days" for enthusiasts.

Slowly, a shift happened.

Customers started requesting him by name.
Other dealerships even noticed his posts.
His income grew — but so did his impact and satisfaction.

Tom wasn't just another salesperson anymore.

He was a high-end brand.

What This Chapter Teaches:

- Your brand is your story, the story people tell when they think of you.

- Building a personal brand leads to loyal customers, repeat business, and endless referrals.

- You don't need to be famous, you just need to be known for something valuable.

Stand for something specific. Serve people passionately.

Tell a story worth repeating.

Reflection: What's Your Personal Brand?

Buyers today aren't just asking,
"What car should I buy?"
They're asking,
"Who do I trust to guide me?"

Your personal brand answers that question before they even ask it.

Your Maven Move: "Define Your Personal Brand"

Exercise:

Ask yourself:

1. What Are You Passionate About?

- High-performance vehicles?
- Family safety and comfort?
- Electric and hybrid innovations?
- Luxury experiences?

    Find the category or mission that lights you up.

2. What Makes You Unique?

- Are you exceptional at explaining technical concepts simply?
- Are you naturally gifted at calming nervous first-time buyers?
- Do you bring humor, energy, professionalism, or patience that others don't?

Own your edge.

3. What Do You Want Customers to Remember?

- Your ability to make car buying easy and fun?
- Your expertise on maintenance and long-term ownership?
- Your genuine investment in their satisfaction?

Craft the experience you want them to talk about.

4. What Value Can You Offer?

- Free car care tips?
- Local driving advice?
- Upgrades and customization advice?

Make yourself useful even after the sale.

Once you have these answers, start telling your story consistently and confidently.

Online.

In person.

In every interaction.

Accountability Action Plan

Action	Goal
Define Your Brand	Write your personal brand statement: passion + expertise + promise.
Create Content	Start posting or sharing 1–2 pieces of helpful content each week (social media, email, dealership blogs).
Reflect Your Brand in Sales Interactions	Mention your expertise naturally in conversations. Reinforce your brand with every customer.
Ask for Feedback	After sales, ask customers how they would describe their experience with you — adjust and refine.
Track Results	Monitor your sales, follow-ups, and referrals to see how your brand is building momentum.

Your brand isn't a logo. It's your reputation in motion.

Reflection / Self-Assessment

- How am I currently perceived by buyers?

- Do I leave a clear, memorable impression or do I blend into the background?

- What three words would I want a customer to use to describe me?

- How can I start living those words more intentionally every day?

Chapter 12

Mastering the Art of Closing the Deal

"Closing the deal is not just about asking for the sale. It's about guiding your customer to a decision that makes them feel confident, valued, and excited about their choice."

Closing isn't about pressure.
It's about partnership.

You're not forcing a decision. You're helping buyers find the moment where everything feels right.

A confident close is built on trust, clear value, and great timing.

When you close correctly, your customer leaves with more than a car, they leave with confidence.

Closing with Confidence

David was a natural relationship-builder.

Customers liked him.
They trusted him.
They loved working with him.

But David had a problem, he hesitated when it came time to close.

- He answered questions.
- He explained features.
- He made buyers feel comfortable.

But when it was time to ask for the sale, David froze, worried about seeming too pushy.

One afternoon, a couple came in looking for a luxury SUV.
They had narrowed it down to two models.

David had walked them through features.
 He had answered every question.

The buyers were at the desk ready to sign.
But hesitation crept in.

David could feel it.

This time, instead of retreating into silence, he leaned in gently and asked:

"What's the one thing holding you back from making a decision today?"

It opened the door.

The customer voiced a fear about value and pricing.

David calmly reframed the conversation:

- He summarized the full value of the car: maintenance packages, future savings, lifestyle fit.
- He offered an exclusive, time-sensitive promotion without sounding desperate.
- He emphasized how the SUV directly met all their stated priorities.
- He concluded with the "Return" option.

The buyers smiled.

The pens came out.

The deal was closed confidently and comfortably.

And David realized:

"Closing isn't about pressure, it's about helping people recognize the right moment to say yes."

What This Chapter Teaches:

- Closing is an extension of the trust you build early on.
- You don't force decisions, you facilitate clarity.
- Understanding concerns and creating urgency without pressure are critical skills.
- A great closing experience leaves customers excited, relieved, and proud of their choice.

What's Your Closing Style?

Think about your approach:

Do you hesitate?
Do you try to rush the close?
Or do you guide the customer confidently to the right decision?

Every conversation you have builds toward that final moment.

Your Maven Move: "Perfecting Your Closing Technique"

Exercise:

Focus on improving your close with these simple strategies:

1. Summarize the Benefits

> Before asking for the sale, take a moment to recap what matters most to the buyer.
>
> Example:
> *"This SUV gives you the safety for your family, the fuel economy you wanted, and the luxury upgrades you deserve. It's the perfect match for where life's taking you next."*

2. Use the Assumptive Close

> Assume the buyer is ready because you've already aligned the value.
>
> Example:
> *"Would you like to take delivery tomorrow, or would next week be better for you?"*

Small assumptive questions build momentum toward yes.

3. Handle Objections with Confidence

Objections aren't rejections, they're invitations to clarify.

Example:
"I completely understand your concern about price. Let's look at the savings built into the maintenance package and warranty coverage over the next five years, this actually saves you thousands."

Always reframe back to value, not price.

4. Create Urgency (Without Pressure)

Make acting today feel smart not stressful.

Example:
"We have this model available with promotional financing until the end of the week. I'd love for you to lock in those savings if this is the right fit for you."

Real urgency respects the customer's decision timeline — and still motivates action.

Accountability Action Plan

Action	Goal
Master a Closing Technique	Pick one close (summary, assumptive, urgency-based) and practice it this week.
Prepare for Objections	Role-play or record yourself responding to 3 common objections.
Introduce Urgency Thoughtfully	Mention special offers or limited inventory calmly and clearly.
Follow-Up Post-Close	Send a personal thank-you call or note after every deal. Reinforce buyer confidence.

Track your success, notice how much smoother your closes feel when you build clarity, not pressure.

Reflection / Self-Assessment

- How do I feel during closing conversations? Confident, nervous, hesitant?

- What objection tends to throw me off balance and how can I better prepare for it?

- Am I giving my buyers reasons to say yes or making them work too hard to decide?

Every great closer asks better questions and listens carefully for the real answer.

Chapter 13
Building Long-Term Relationships for Repeat Business

"A sale isn't the end of a relationship — it's the beginning of a partnership that can last for years."

The most valuable customer is not the one who buys once.
It's the one who buys again and brings their friends, family, and coworkers with them.

Every interaction either builds or breaks long-term loyalty.

When you treat every buyer like the start of a lifelong relationship, you don't have to chase the next sale, it comes to you.

From One Sale to a Lifetime of Referrals

Maria had just purchased her first car from Mark, a seasoned salesperson.

The experience had been smooth.
Maria felt confident.

But it was what happened after the sale that really made the difference.

One week later, Maria received a simple, thoughtful message:

"Hi Maria, just checking in to make sure you're loving your new car.
If you have any questions or need anything, I'm here for you!"

It wasn't a pitch.
It wasn't a survey.

It was care.

Maria had a few questions about the car's features. Mark answered them patiently and even scheduled her a free car wash and a complimentary maintenance check-up.

Over the next several months:

- He sent gentle maintenance reminders.
- He checked in around holidays.
- He offered small but relevant tips like prepping the car for winter.

A year later, Maria was ready for her next vehicle.

She didn't shop around.
She didn't compare dealerships.

She called—Mark was her guy.

And this time, she brought her sister too.

One sale had grown into two — and the referrals kept coming.

Because Mark understood:
"The first sale isn't the goal — it's the foundation."

What This Chapter Teaches:

- A closed deal is just the beginning of a long-term relationship.
- Customers who feel valued become loyal repeat buyers and enthusiastic referrers.
- Simple, authentic follow-ups, personalization, and ongoing value drive loyalty.
- It's easier and smarter to keep a customer than to constantly chase new ones.

Reflection: Are You Ready to Be the Go-To Person?

Think about your process:

Do you treat every buyer like a future relationship or just today's transaction?
Do you have a system for staying in touch after the sale?
What small gestures could you add to turn satisfaction into loyalty?

Loyalty isn't bought — it's earned and nurtured.

Your Maven Move: "Turning One-Time Sales into Lifetime Relationships"

Exercise:

Focus on building deeper, longer-lasting connections with every customer using these strategies:

1. Follow Up Within 48 Hours

> Send a personalized thank-you call, text, or email within two days of delivery.

Ask:

- "How are you loving your new car?"
- "Any questions I can answer now that you've had a few days with it?"

Speed + sincerity = trust reinforcement.

2. Create a Personalized Experience

    Take notes on buyer conversations.

    Remember details like:

    - Family members.
    - Hobbies.
    - Upcoming life events (e.g., new baby, new job).

    Use these moments to send relevant, thoughtful messages later.

3. Offer Value Beyond the Sale

    Share:

- Maintenance tips.
- Recall alerts.
- Warranty extension reminders.
- Invitations to VIP service days or free car clinics.

Help buyers protect and enjoy their vehicle — not just buy it.

4. Stay in Touch Regularly

Calendar important touchpoints:

- 3- and 6-month check-in.
- Birthday greetings.
- Anniversary of their car purchase.

Small surprises mean big loyalty.

5. Ask for Referrals (The Right Way)

Accountability Action Plan

Action	Goal
48-Hour Follow-Up	Reach out personally to every new buyer within 48 hours of purchase.
Customer Notes	Track personal details (family, hobbies, future needs) in your CRM or notebook.
Ongoing Touchpoints	Calendar a system to reconnect at 3 months, 6 months, and 1 year.
Referral System	Set a monthly referral goal and recognize referrers meaningfully.
Review Experience	Regularly ask: *"How can I improve my post-sale experience?"*

Make long-term loyalty your daily priority, not just an afterthought.

Reflection / Self-Assessment

- How am I currently following up after a sale?//
- What touchpoints can I add to show buyers they're valued after they drive off the lot?
- How can I surprise and delight customers when they least expect it?

Loyalty doesn't happen by luck, it happens by care.

Chapter 14

Leveraging Social Media for Sales Success

"Social media is the digital handshake that opens the door to new opportunities. It's not just about selling cars; it's about building relationships that last."

In today's world, buyers are making decisions long before they walk into the dealership.
They're researching.
They're comparing.
They're watching.

Your online presence is your first impression — and sometimes your only chance to connect.

Use social media not just to showcase cars, but to showcase you, your knowledge, your care, your credibility.

Building a Personal Brand on Social Media

Tasha was a talented car salesperson with strong people skills.

She closed deals.
She earned referrals.

But she knew she could reach more buyers if she found a way to connect outside the dealership walls.

After researching how others built personal brands, she made a decision:

She would build her own online presence.

Tasha started simple:

- She set up a clean, professional LinkedIn profile highlighting her auto expertise.

- She created Instagram and Facebook accounts focused on car education and customer success stories.

- She posted car-buying tips, customer celebrations, dealership moments, and behind-the-scenes content.

But Tasha didn't just post, she engaged:

- She answered questions in comments.

- She congratulated buyers online.

- She DM'ed helpful advice to first-time buyers.

Over time, something incredible happened:

- Buyers reached out to her directly.
- They asked for advice.
- They trusted her before they even met her.

Within a few months, Tasha's sales numbers doubled.

She became *"the car expert"* in her community, not because of a bigger showroom, but because of a bigger presence.

What This Chapter Teaches:

- Social media is relationship-building at scale.
- It allows you to earn trust before the first handshake.
- A strong, consistent online presence increases visibility, credibility, and loyalty.
- Buyers today want to know the person behind the product and social media is the best place to show them.

How Can You Start Building Your Social Media Presence?

Think about your strategy:

Are you visible online?
Are you offering value — or just promotions?
Are you creating opportunities for buyers to know you — and trust you — before they even step into the dealership?

Buyers today choose people before they choose products.

Your Maven Move: "Using Social Media to Increase Your Sales"

Exercise:

Use these steps to start building your powerful social media presence:

1. Choose Your Platforms Wisely

>   Pick 1–2 platforms to start with.

- LinkedIn for professionalism and business network building.
- Instagram for visual engagement.
- Facebook for community awareness and broader audience reach.

Set up complete, professional profiles that highlight:

- Your expertise.
- Your dealership (subtly).
- Your customer-first mindset.

2. Post Valuable, Relatable Content

Ideas for posts:

- Car-buying tips (e.g., "Top 3 Mistakes First-Time Buyers Make").
- Behind-the-scenes dealership life.
- New model arrivals or test drives.
- Customer delivery celebrations (with permission!).
- Quick financing FAQs.

- "Did You Know?" car facts or maintenance tips.

Consistency is key — aim for 3–4 posts per week.

3. Engage Authentically

Social media isn't a billboard — it's a conversation.

Respond thoughtfully:

- Like, comment, and reply to your followers.
- Answer questions in DMs.
- Share useful tips when you see buyers asking for advice.

Build real relationships, not just a following.

4. Share Success Stories and Testimonials

Share photos (with permission) and stories of happy buyers: "Congratulations to Sarah on her first car purchase! Proud to be part of her journey!"

Nothing builds trust like real people and real smiles.

5. Use Hashtags and Location Tags

Increase visibility with hashtags like:

- #CarBuyingTips
- #NewCarDay
- #YourCityName
- #CarGoals
- #DealershipLife

Always tag your dealership location and your city.

Be discoverable to buyers nearby who are already looking for help.

6. Create Videos and Go Live

Videos build faster trust than photos or text alone.

Easy video ideas:

- Quick car tours.

- Feature highlights.
- 60-second financing tip.
- FAQ answers.
- "Meet your salesperson" casual intro.

Live sessions (even short ones!) make you real and relatable.

Accountability Action Plan

Action	Goal
Social Media Schedule	Commit to posting 3–4 times per week. Plan posts ahead if needed.
Daily Engagement	Comment, answer questions, and DM helpful replies to build community daily.
Content Tracking	Track what posts get the most engagement and double down on what works.
Exclusive Online Promotions	Offer at least one special offer through social media monthly.
Measure Results	Track how many inquiries, test drives, and sales come from your online efforts over 30–60 days.

Start small. Stay consistent. It's about momentum. Grow your online handshake into lifelong buyer relationships.

Reflection / Self-Assessment

- What would someone learn about me if they found my Instagram, LinkedIn, or Facebook page today?

- Am I giving buyers reasons to trust me before we meet?

- How can I show more value, humanity, and expertise in my online presence?

Online visibility isn't vanity, it's velocity.

Chapter 15
Mastering the Test Drive

"The test drive is not just about driving a car; it's about driving a connection with your customer."

The test drive is your ultimate closing tool — but only if you make it personal.

It's not just about the specs. It's about the spark.

When buyers feel the car fits into their life — emotionally and practically — the decision becomes easy.

Turning the Test Drive into a Personal Experience

John had been dealership-hopping for weeks.
He read reviews.
He compared models online.

But he still hadn't felt that moment, that feeling that this was the right car.

Then he met Sarah.

Instead of rushing him to the driver's seat, Sarah paused and asked:

"What's most important to you when you drive? Comfort? Handling? Technology?"

John felt seen.
John felt heard.

During the drive, Sarah didn't just rattle off features.

She asked:

- *"How's the steering feel?"*
- *"Is the cabin quiet enough for you?"*
- *"Can you picture yourself driving this on your daily route?"*

She pointed out safety features only after John showed interest — not before.

Sarah matched the experience to John's life, not a checklist.

By the time they pulled back into the lot, John wasn't just sold on the car, he was sold on the experience.

And he bought the car that day, because it felt personal, not pressured.

What This Chapter Teaches:

- The test drive is an emotional moment, not just a technical one.
- Buyers often decide during the drive based on feel, not facts.
- Tailoring the drive to the customer's lifestyle builds connection, trust, and comfort.
- The salesperson who connects the car to the customer's *real world* wins.

Reflection: How Do You Approach Test Drives?

Are you making the test drive about the customer or about the car?
Are you asking questions that uncover emotions or just quoting features?
Are you listening for subtle cues that show excitement or hesitation?

Great salespeople read the road between the words.

Your Maven Move: "Maximizing the Test Drive to Close the Deal"

Exercise:

- "What matters most to you when you drive?"
- "What do you wish your last car had done better?"
- "What's your ideal driving experience like?"

Accountability Action Plan

Action	Goal
Pre-Drive Interview	Ask 3 discovery questions before every test drive.
Personalized Route	Customize each drive route when possible based on buyer needs.
Highlight Emotion, Not Specs	Focus on how the car fits their lifestyle, not just stats.
Track Test Drive Closures	Track how many test drives lead to next steps or closes. Analyze why.
Follow Up Within 24 Hours	Send a personalized thank-you message after every test drive, even if they don't buy that day.

Make the test drive about them, not you — and watch your conversions soar.

Reflection / Self-Assessment

- How personal are my test drives today?
- Am I showcasing the car or showcasing the buyer's future?
- What simple change could I make tomorrow to create a more emotional, memorable test drive?

When buyers feel the car fits their life, the paperwork is just a formality.

Chapter 16
Overcoming Objections and Closing the Deal

"Objections are not the enemy of a sale; they're the gateway to providing more value and building deeper trust."

Objections aren't the end — they're the beginning of deeper conversation.

Every concern a customer raises is a clue to what matters most to them.

Great salespeople don't bulldoze objections. They build bridges with them.

Turning an Objection Into a Sale

Eric had been working with Lisa for over an hour.
She loved the SUV.
She loved the features.

But then came the hesitation:

"I'm just not sure it fits into my budget..."

Eric didn't flinch.
He didn't push.
He didn't rush to discount.

Instead, he said simply:

"What's your budget range, Lisa? I completely understand wanting to stay within your comfort zone."

By listening carefully and respecting her concern, Eric uncovered the real issue:

Lisa wasn't walking away because she didn't like the car, she was afraid of stretching too far financially.

Instead of forcing the original SUV, Eric:

- Showed a few similar models that fit her budget.
- Explained creative financing options.
- Focused on value over price.

Lisa didn't feel "sold to."
She felt heard, respected, and guided.

And she bought — happily.

What This Chapter Teaches:

- Objections are buyer's signals, not rejection.
- Every concern is a window into the buyer's priorities, fears, or needs.
- Active listening + flexible solutions = trust, loyalty, and closing power.
- Mastering objections is mastering human connection, not memorizing rebuttals.

Reflection: How Do You Handle Objections?

Do you listen patiently or start formulating your comeback immediately?

Do you validate concerns or accidentally minimize them?

Do you guide toward solutions or default to lowering price?

How you handle objections defines how your buyers feel when they leave.

Your Maven Move: "Turning Objections Into Opportunities"

Exercise:

Use these steps to transform objections into successful sales conversations:

1. Listen Actively and Fully

    When an objection surfaces:

    - Stop.
    - Lean in.
    - Let them finish.

    Your calm attention alone will often lower their defensiveness immediately.

2. Acknowledge and Validate

    Affirm their concern respectfully:

    - "That's a really fair point."
    - "I'm glad you shared that with me — it's important."
    - "I understand where you're coming from."

Validation builds emotional safety.

3. Ask Clarifying Questions

Examples:

- "What part of the offer feels like the biggest hurdle?"
- "Is it more about monthly payments, overall cost, or something else?"
- "If we could solve that piece, would this otherwise feel right?"

Dig deeper without pressure.

4. Offer Alternative Solutions

Tailor your response:

- Show similar vehicles.
- Offer financing or leasing solutions.
- Highlight cost-of-ownership savings.
- Emphasize the "Return" or loyalty incentives.

Be flexible and resourceful — not defensive.

5. Use the Trial Close

If they're close but hesitant, gently test readiness:

"If we can find a solution for this concern, would you be ready to move forward today?"

Trial closes show you're listening — and that you're ready to help.

6. Close with Calm Confidence

When the moment feels right:

- Summarize how their concerns were addressed.
- Reaffirm their wise decision.
- Invite them into action confidently:

"Let's make sure you're leaving today feeling excited and secure about your choice."

Confidence — without pressure — seals the trust.

Accountability Action Plan

Action	Goal
Identify Top 5 Objections	List the five most common objections you hear. Create 2–3 empathetic, solution-oriented responses for each.
Practice Active Listening Daily	In every buyer conversation, practice listening for at least 60 seconds before offering any solutions.
Role Play Objection Handling	Set up weekly practice with a teammate — alternate roles and refine your calm, confident responses.
Track Objection Resolutions	Track which objections you overcome most successfully. Analyze why. Adjust strategies for tougher ones.
Celebrate Wins	Every time you turn an objection into a sale, reflect: *What worked? What built trust? What can I repeat?*

Objections are not interruptions.

Objections are invitations to deeper trust.

Reflection / Self-Assessment

- How quickly do I jump to solutions versus fully understanding the buyer's concerns?

- What emotional signals do I notice when objections arise in myself and in the customer?

- How could I make my objection handling less defensive and more partnership-driven?

When buyers feel you're fighting for them, not against them, the sale becomes a shared victory.

Bonus Chapter
Master the Follow-Up — Forever

"The sale ends on paper — but the relationship is just beginning."

Following up isn't extra work, it's the heart of long-term sales success.

A single sale can turn into five if you master the art of thoughtful, consistent connection.

Every time you reach out with care, you're planting seeds for future growth.

What This Bonus Chapter Reiterates:

- The sale is not the finish line, it's the start of a journey.
- Most buyers forget their salesperson within 90 days unless you stay relevant.
- Strategic follow-up turns one satisfied buyer into a lifetime of referrals and repeat business.
- Consistency beats intensity — small touchpoints, done regularly, create massive results.

Reflection: What's Your Follow-Up Strategy?

Are you following up because you genuinely care or only when you want something?
Are you staying visible without being overly assertive?
Are you offering value after the sale — or are you disappearing?

The fortune isn't just in the follow-up, it's in the way you follow up.

Your Maven Move: "The Follow-Up Forever System"

Here's a simple, powerful Scripts + Schedule + Strategy guide you can implement today:

1. Follow-Up Scripts (Templates You Can Use)

> **48 Hours After Sale — Check-In Message**
> *"Hi [Customer Name], just checking in! Hope you're loving your new [Car Model]. Let me know if you have any questions — I'm here for you anytime."*

1 Week After Sale — Value Add

"Hey [Customer Name], quick tip: did you know your [Car Model]'s [Feature] can [Benefit]? Let me know if you'd like a quick walkthrough!"

1 Month After Sale — Loyalty Building

"It's been a month already! How's everything going with your new [Car Model]? Remember, I'm still your go-to for any car questions or future needs."

Birthday or Special Occasion

"Happy Birthday, [Customer Name]! Wishing you an amazing year ahead. Thanks again for trusting me with your [Car Model] journey!"

Service Reminder (3-6 Months After Sale)

"Just a heads-up — it might be time for your first service on the [Car Model]. Let me know if you need any help scheduling!"

Annual Anniversary

"Can you believe it's been a year with your [Car Model]? Thanks again for being an awesome part of our dealership family. Let's keep your vehicle running strong!"

2. Follow-Up Schedule (Simple Calendar Blueprint)

Timing	Purpose
48 Hours	Confirm satisfaction, answer immediate questions.
1 Week	Reinforce value, share helpful tips.
1 Month	Build loyalty, open the door for referrals.
3–6 Months	Offer service reminders or upgrades.
Birthday or Holidays	Personalize connection, build goodwill.
1 Year Anniversary	Celebrate milestones, refresh relationship.

Consistency beats frequency.
Be visible — but never annoying.

3. Follow-Up Strategies (How to Stay Meaningful)

Personalization Always Wins

Mention their family, their job, or a moment from the sale. *"Hope the new [Car Model] is helping with those school runs you mentioned!"*

Give Value Before You Ask for Anything

Share maintenance tips, local events, warranty reminders, things that help them, even when you're not selling.

Use Multiple Channels

Alternate between text, handwritten notes, emails, and occasional calls. Keep it human and natural.

Track It All

Use a simple CRM, spreadsheet, or even a calendar app to set follow-up reminders and log responses.

Ask for Referrals — Gently

After checking in, add: *"If you know someone who needs a car, I'd love to offer them the same great experience!"*

Accountability Action Plan

Action	Goal
Create Your Follow-Up Templates	Write or save your scripts today. Make them easy to personalize.
Set Up a Simple Tracking System	CRM, Excel, or Google Calendar — doesn't matter. Just track who, when, and why you followed up.
Commit to Daily Follow-Ups	Reach out to 2–3 past customers daily. Small steps build massive results over time.
Review and Adjust Monthly	What's working? What isn't? Tweak your scripts and schedule to stay fresh and valuable.

Following up isn't chasing — it's continuing the relationship you started on the lot. Commit to it!

Reflection / Self-Assessment

- How many past customers are in your follow-up system today?

- How many meaningful connections could you create with just 5–10 minutes a day?

- What would happen to your referrals and repeat sales if you became *the salesperson who never forgets?*

Master the follow-up and you master your future.

Closing Chapter
The Daily Commitment to Mastery

"The sale ends on paper — but the journey of mastery is just beginning."

True success isn't built on one big moment, it's built on small, powerful decisions made daily.

Mastery is not an achievement. It's a habit.

Start today. Start small. Stay committed.

The Power of a New Day

I start every morning with two simple things, anything that drives and motivates you:

- An encouraging verse.
- A powerful quote.
- A phone call.

Why?
Because how you start the day sets the tone for everything that follows.

In sales and in life, your attitude is contagious.
A positive mindset attracts better conversations, better opportunities, and better outcomes.

As Robert Collier reminds us:

"Success is the sum of small efforts, repeated day in and day out."

Each small action is significant.
Each conversation shapes your reputation.
Each buyer interaction builds or erodes trust.

You are not just selling cars.
You are building a career, a legacy, and a life of influence.

The Power of Consistency and Mastery

The best salespeople aren't the ones who know every feature or memorize every rebate.
The best are those who commit daily to improving their craft, one skill, one conversation, one interaction at a time.

Start small: Pick one tool or technique from this book each day.

Focus deeply: Practice it, refine it, master it.
Build momentum: Progress compounds faster than perfection.

Become Significant.

Today's small win becomes tomorrow's transformation.

Your Ongoing Commitment to Growth

When you keep this handbook nearby not buried in a drawer, but active in your day-to-day work it becomes more than just pages.
It becomes your accountability partner.
It becomes your proof that you are serious about success.
It becomes a silent, powerful symbol to your buyers:
"I am someone who never stops improving for you."

And trust me, your customers will notice.

When they see you still growing, still learning, still showing up with excellence, still caring.
They trust you more.
They send their friends to you.
They stay loyal for life.

Reflection: Your True Measure of Success

Success isn't measured by the number of deals you close this month.

It's measured by the number of people who leave your lot better, happier, and more cared for because you were the one who helped them. Be a difference maker.

Each handshake.
Each test drive.
Each smile.
Each "thank you."

These moments matter.
They create ripples far beyond the showroom.

You are not just selling cars,
You are changing lives.
You are easing fears.
You are building dreams.

Your Maven Move: "Daily Commitment to Mastery"

Action Plan for Daily Success:

1. Start Each Day with Purpose

- Begin your morning by reading a motivational quote or uplifting verse.
- Set a personal goal: *"Today, I will listen better." "Today, I will handle objections with more empathy." "Today, I will perfect my test drive walkthrough."*

2. Focus on One Skill Each Day

- Pick one specific technique from this handbook.
- Practice it intentionally with every customer you meet.

3. Track Your Growth

   Keep a simple daily journal:
   - *What worked well today?*
   - *What challenged me?*
   - *What can I improve tomorrow?*

   Progress, not perfection, is the goal.

4. Reinforce Your Commitment Publicly

> Share your growth mindset with your customers: *"I'm always learning, always striving to serve you better."*
>
> Professionalism + humility builds unstoppable loyalty.

Your Accountability Challenge

Starting tomorrow, challenge yourself:
One customer. One action. One improvement. Everyday.

Small steps, repeated consistently, build unstoppable mastery.

Final Words of Wisdom

"The best way to predict your future is to create it."
— Abraham Lincoln

You have everything you need:

- The skills.

- The mindset.
- The opportunity.

Now, it's time to create the future you deserve, one day, one conversation, one choice at a time.

Congratulations!

You have completed *How to Sell Cars: The Art of the Dealership*.

You now have the tools, the knowledge, and the commitment to build a remarkable career based on trust, authenticity, and excellence. Your income level and growth potential is waiting for you — Reach for it!

Keep showing up.
Keep growing.
Keep rewriting the future of automotive sales.

See you tomorrow — as Day 1 of your Accountability Challenge begins.

— Your Future Self

30-Day Sales Challenge
Building Lasting Habits and Accountability

Welcome to your 30-Day Sales Challenge. This challenge is designed to help you take action, build lasting habits, and put the techniques from this guide into practice. By focusing on small, achievable goals each day, you'll create powerful habits that will transform your sales process and elevate your customer relationships.

Throughout this challenge, you'll focus on one key concept each day, allowing repetition to reinforce the habits and techniques that will lead you to success. Every day, take the time to reflect on your progress and make adjustments as needed. At the end of the 30 days, you'll be amazed at the growth you've achieved.

How the Challenge Works:

- Daily Focus: Each day has a specific task, technique, or behavior to master.

- Action: Every day, commit to completing the task and using the technique in your customer interactions.

- Reflection: At the end of the day, take a moment to reflect on what worked, what didn't, and how you can improve.

- Accountability: Check in with yourself each day. If you have a colleague or manager to share your progress with, that's even better. You can also use a journal to track your daily wins and challenges.

Day 1: Setting Your Intention

Task: Write down your goals for the next 30 days. What do you want to achieve in terms of sales and customer relationships? Commit to this challenge fully.

Reflection: What is your "why"? Why do you want to improve as a salesperson? How does this challenge fit into your larger career goals?

_____

_____

_____

Day 2: Perfecting Your First Impression

Task: Practice your greeting and introduction. When meeting a customer, focus on making a strong first impression with a warm, friendly, and confident approach.

Reflection: How did the customer respond to your introduction? Were you able to establish rapport right away?

_____

_____

_____

Day 3: Active Listening

Task: Focus on listening more than talking. When a customer speaks, truly listen to their needs, desires, and concerns without interrupting.

Reflection: Did you learn something new about your customer by truly listening? How did it change the direction of the conversation?

_____

_____

_____

Day 4: Asking Open-Ended Questions

Task: Practice asking open-ended questions to discover your customer's true needs. Ask questions like, "What is most important to you in a car?" or "How do you plan to use your vehicle?"

Reflection: Did your questions reveal more about your customer's needs and preferences? How did it shape the conversation?

_____

_____

_____

Day 5: Building Rapport

Task: Work on connecting with your customer on a personal level. Find common ground, whether it's about their lifestyle, hobbies, or something else.

Reflection: Did you establish a personal connection? What did you learn about them? How did it affect the customer's willingness to engage with you?

_____

_____

_____

Day 6: Handling Objections - Part 1

Task: When a customer raises an objection, acknowledge their concern and ask for more details. Practice reframing objections as opportunities to provide additional value.

Reflection: How did you handle the objection? Did you find a way to address it while reinforcing the value of your product?

_____

_____

_____

Day 7: Following Up

Task: Practice following up with at least one potential customer. Use the phone, email, or text to check in and offer more assistance.

Reflection: How did the follow-up go? Were you able to provide additional value or information that moved the customer closer to making a decision?

_____

_____

_____

Day 8: Using the Power of Body Language

Task: Focus on your body language. Ensure that your posture, eye contact, and gestures convey confidence, openness, and attentiveness.

Reflection: How did the customer react to your body language? Did it help establish a stronger connection?

_____

_____

_____

Day 9: Mastering the Art of the Close

Task: Practice a variety of closing techniques. Focus on matching the closing style to the customer's personality. Try the assumptive close, the alternative close, or the summary close.

Reflection: Which closing technique felt most natural to you? Did you feel more confident closing a deal today?

_____

_____

_____

Day 10: Learning to Let Go

Task: After a customer decision is made (whether a sale or not), learn to let go gracefully. Thank them for their time and leave the door open for future business.

Reflection: How did you handle the interaction after the sale or no-sale? Did you feel confident in your ability to maintain a positive relationship?

_____

_____

_____

Day 11: Staying Organized

Task: Implement a simple system to track customer interactions and follow-ups. Whether it's a spreadsheet, a CRM tool, or a notebook, keep track of your leads and follow-ups.

Reflection: Did you feel more in control of your time today? How did staying organized affect your sales process?

_____

_____

_____

Day 12: Personalizing Your Sales Pitch

Task: Customize your sales pitch to each customer based on what you've learned about them so far. Make your pitch about how the vehicle fits their specific needs, not just a generic overview.

Reflection: How did your personalized pitch resonate with the customer? Did they seem more engaged?

_____

_____

_____

Day 13: Providing Solutions, Not Just Products

Task: Frame your vehicle as a solution to your customers' problems. Focus on how it will improve their daily life or address a pain point they've shared with you.

Reflection: Did your approach feel more consultative? Did you notice any difference in how the customer responded?

_____

_____

_____

Day 14: Handling Objections - Part 2

Task: Practice handling more difficult objections. Use empathy to understand their concerns and provide thoughtful, well-reasoned responses.

Reflection: How did your approach change with tougher objections? What did you learn from the experience?

_____

_____

_____

Day 15: Keeping a Positive Attitude

Task: Maintain a positive attitude regardless of the situation. Whether you're facing rejection or celebrating a success, keep your energy level high.

Reflection: How did staying positive influence your interactions today? Did it affect the customer's perception of you?

_____

_____

_____

Day 16: Strengthening Your Product Knowledge

Task: Deepen your understanding of the vehicles you sell. Spend some time researching features, benefits, and the unique selling points of your inventory.

Reflection: How did your enhanced product knowledge impact your conversations with customers? Did it build more trust?

_____

_____

_____

Day 17: Practicing Empathy

Task: Focus on empathizing with your customers' concerns and emotions. Acknowledge their feelings and validate their point of view.

Reflection: Did practicing empathy create a more meaningful connection with your customer? How did it influence their decision-making?

_____

_____

_____

Day 18: Reflecting on Your Successes

Task: Take a moment to reflect on the successes you've had so far. Celebrate the wins, no matter how small, and acknowledge how far you've come in just 18 days.

Reflection: What have been your biggest wins so far? How has your confidence grown since starting this challenge?

_____

_____

_____

Day 19: Overcoming Fear of Rejection

Task: Take a deep breath and approach a customer who you fear might say no. Practice handling rejection gracefully and moving on to the next opportunity.

Reflection: How did you feel after facing rejection? Did it affect your attitude toward future sales?

_____

_____

_____

Day 20: Building Trust

Task: Work on establishing trust with your customer. Be transparent, honest, and always follow through on your promises.

Reflection: How did the customer react to your honesty? Did you feel a stronger bond being formed?

_____

_____

_____

Day 21: Sharing Your Expertise

Task: Offer your expertise by sharing valuable advice with your customers, whether it's related to financing options, vehicle maintenance, or choosing the right model.

Reflection: Did you notice the customer relying on you for advice? Did it establish you as a trusted resource?

_____

_____

_____

Day 22: Focusing on Customer Service

Task: Go above and beyond in delivering exceptional service. Offer to answer any lingering questions and ensure that the customer feels well taken care of.

Reflection: How did your customer respond to the added service? Did it influence their perception of you and your dealership?

_____

_____

_____

Day 23: Handling Objections - Part 3

Task: Master your final objection-handling technique. Combine all the techniques you've learned to handle objections with grace, tact, and confidence.

Reflection: How did you feel handling objections today? Were you able to turn objections into opportunities for closing?

_____

_____

_____

Day 24: Becoming a Resource, Not Just a Seller

Task: Shift your mindset from salesperson to trusted resource. Think of yourself as someone who is there to provide the best solution, rather than just to sell a vehicle.

Reflection: Did you feel more genuine in your interactions? How did the customer respond to your approach?

_____

_____

_____

Day 25: Recognizing Non-Verbal Cues

Task: Pay attention to the customer's body language, tone of voice, and facial expressions. Use these cues to adjust your approach as needed.

Reflection: What did you learn by tuning in to your customer's non-verbal communication? How did it impact the conversation?

_____

_____

_____

Day 26: Offering Solutions, Not Features

Task: Focus on the benefits your vehicle offers, not just the features. How does the vehicle improve the customer's life or solve a problem?

Reflection: Did the customer seem more engaged with the benefits of the car rather than the technical details?

_____

_____

_____

Day 27: Practicing Patience

Task: Slow down and focus on creating a calm, patient environment. Don't rush the process and give your customer the space they need to make an informed decision.

Reflection: How did slowing down impact your customer interactions? Did it lead to a better connection?

_____

_____

_____

Day 28: Celebrating Your Wins

Task: Take a moment to celebrate your progress so far. Reflect on what you've learned, how much you've grown, and how your mindset has shifted.

Reflection: What are your most significant takeaways from the past 28 days? How will you carry these lessons forward?

_____

_____

_____

Day 29: Refining Your Closing Techniques

Task: Refine your closing techniques based on the experiences of the past month. Focus on the approach that feels most natural to you and practice it until it becomes second nature.

Reflection: Which closing technique worked best for you today? What adjustments can you make going forward?

_____

_____

_____

Day 30: Committing to Long-Term Growth

Task: Commit to continuous improvement. Set new goals for yourself and make a promise to keep building on the habits you've established during this challenge.

Reflection: How will you maintain your growth after the 30-day challenge? What's next for your sales career?

_____

_____

_____

Accountability and Follow-Up

At the end of each day, take five minutes to evaluate your performance. Did you complete the task? Did you feel confident in your actions? Write down any insights or struggles you had and use them as learning opportunities.

www.ingramcontent.com/pod-product-compliance
Lightning Source LLC
Chambersburg PA
CBHW051547010526
44118CB00022B/2607